BUT FO
MEN AS

The Heroes of the Railway Incident at Soham, Cambridgeshire in June 1944

Anthony Day

S.B. Publications

By the same author: *Wicken: A Fen Village* (1990)
Fen and Marshland Villages (1993)

First published in 1994 by S. B. Publications
c/o 19 Grove Road, Seaford, East Sussex BN25 1TP.
Reprinted 1997

ISBN: 1 85770 060 0

Typeset, printed and bound by
Manchester Free Press,
Longford Trading Estate,
Thomas Street, Stretford,
Manchester M32 0JT.
Tel: 061 864 4540.

CONTENTS

Front Cover: The heroes of the Soham incident and the burning wagon as depicted by John Honeywell of Trowbridge in his painting of 1972-74

Title Page: Fireman and acting driver Ben Gimbert (left) earlier in the war *(Joyce Dedman Collection)*

BIBLIOGRAPHY

Brave Railwaymen by Allan Stanistreet
(Token Publishing Limited) 1989

Railway Ghosts by J.A. Brooks
(Jarrold Publishing) 1985

By Rail to Victory: The Story of the L.N.E.R. in Wartime
by Norman Crump (L.N.E.R. Publication) 1947

A Master Miller Remembers by J.P. Clark
as told to Gareth Adamson 1978

Report for the Ministry of War Transport
by Major G.R.S. Wilson, 19th September 1944

The War Incident at Soham, June 2nd 1944
by the Reverend Percy Fletcher Boughey
and Ethel Mary Waldock
(a sixpenny pamphlet published after the war).

ACKNOWLEDGEMENTS

I am grateful to the following, who were my direct sources of information: Joyce and Roland Dedman, Pat Gimbert, Mr and Mrs Gordon Bridges, Dennis Bridges, Jane Hull, Eric Isaacson, Edith King, Ron Barber, Derek Bradley, Edith and Stuart Canham, Ann Jarman, John Gilbey, Arthur Clarke, John Clarke of Washington DC, Pat and Les Seal, Joan and Albert Peacock, Florence Young, Dick Reed, Kathleen Pope, Gladys Turner, Barbara Richmond, Pauline Bambridge and Mike Lamport.

I am indebted to Mike Petty and Chris Jakes of the Cambridgeshire Collection for their help and advice and to Steve Benz of S.B. Publications for welcoming this book.

INTRODUCTION

The title words were spoken by the Reverend Percy Fletcher Boughey in Soham church on Sunday 4th June 1944 in preface to his tribute to the four brave railwaymen who, two days earlier, had saved the town of Soham from virtual destruction. Two had died, one lay critically injured and the fourth damaged in hospital after an otherwise successful and totally selfless attempt to save hundreds of lives.

This was not the address planned by the vicar for his 'Salute the Soldier Week' service but another hastily prepared for a congregation waiting to give thanks for their deliverance. The wounded town was still in shock but its foundations were largely intact and the people were there to mourn the dead heroes and celebrate their own survival.

Fifty years on the names of three of those heroes live on in housing developments and on railway engines and this is an attempt to revive them as people. They are, of course, fondly remembered, relatively young, by their surviving families and friends and it is to them that I am grateful for their patient recollections. The idea for the book came from Jane Hull, a native of Soham, who had accumulated material relating to the incident and had brought it to me some four years ago in anticipation of the fiftieth anniversary. My credentials are disclosed in a memoir of Soham which played such a big part in my upbringing and the rest is devoted to perpetuating the lives of Benjamin Gimbert, James Nightall, Frank Bridges and Herbert Clarke for future generations, for such lives should never be forgotten.

Soham Mere, painted by Vernet, engraved by C.J. Beck in the 1700s
(Cambridgeshire Collection)

1. A MEMOIR OF SOHAM

We were living no more than half-a-mile away by the footpath, or four miles round by cycle or bus and it offered most of what we needed of town life in goods, services and entertainment while embodying the spirit of community and celebration. Soham was my paternal grandmother's home, the firstborn of John and Eliza Bradley, nee Beeton, who having married George Day lived a farmer's wife in Wicken, bearing seven children. Thereafter for many years George took out his pony and buggy on Thursdays to go via Soham to Ely Market, leaving his wife and pre-school children with her family and going on to Ely by train.

We called it the smallest town or the largest village in England, accessible to me from infancy, where the speech was indistinguishable from our own, where 'ye' was still being used for 'you' and 'housen' for 'houses' in my childhood between the wars and others ways of speaking grated on our ears. A town it was along the main concourse, but not far away was the ripe rural atmosphere of home where grandma's brothers had become farmers too. My mother soon grew close to them and we visited often, enjoying also the shops and the recreation ground with its swings and slide and the lift-off to the seaside once a year from that little well-equipped station, climbing on board our own village on wheels for a magical journey. Children today could hardly behold a diesel electric locomotive as we beheld that sizzling leviathan waiting to expend its power for our pleasure, thrusting in huge breaths into the blue.

Soham people were such evident home-lovers, happily insular, and they were never likely to use that station to venture too far away for long. It was opened there on 1st September 1879, serving the Ely-Fordham-Newmarket line covering thirteen-and-a-half miles. Then in 1898 it was absorbed by the Great Eastern Railway and then, in 1938, due to the increasing amount of produce coming off the fens for transit, the London and North Eastern Railway double-tracked the six miles between Soham and Snailwell Junction. It stood seventy-five-and-a-half miles from London, nineteen north-

An old print depicting Soham in the 1840s.
(Cambridgeshire Collection)

Soham Mere drainage mill in August 1929. Built by Soham millwright, Thomas Hunt in the 1860s, it was a relic of another age when demolished by the use of gelignite in 1948. Vermuiden's drainage scheme depended on such means of lifting water.
(Cambridgeshire Collection)

east from Cambridge, eight north-west from Newmarket and six south-east from Ely.

This in the Hundred of Staploe, rural district and petty sessional division of Newmarket, county court district of Ely, rural deanery of Fordham and archdeaconry and diocese of Ely. While we in the smaller parishes lit our way by paraffin and warmed our home with turf, coal or logs, Soham had its gas works near the station, the property of the Soham and District Gas Company, and was partly supplied with electricity by the Bedfordshire, Cambridgeshire and Huntingdonshire Electricity Company. The access roads had been good for a long time, ours following the winding route along the highest elevation and Soham Lode, arriving from Snailwell and joining the Great Ouse past the hamlet of Barway, was navigable and still conveying fen produce, coal and timber.

Long ago there was the mere separating our two communities. Some of it was drained between 1594 and 1600 but when Vermuiden's great drainage scheme extended to the whole of the mere there were uprisings against it from those who had depended on its resources of fish, wildfowl, reeds and sedge. Spades, poles, stones and pitchforks were the weapons and on May 1st 1637 the local Justices of the Peace were urged to be severe on the obstructors of the scheme. It is likely the name Soham came from that mere — 'Ham by the lake.'

During my childhood and closest affiliation with Soham the population remained under five thousand in a parish that possessed 12,946 acres of land and 53 of water. We in Wicken knew its tradesmen so well, for they brought all the news when they did their rounds of our village, thus forcing our own tradesmen to travel outwards. There came weekly those representatives of Waddington's and Walker's Stores, the grocers, and little Mr Bird whose shop was on the corner of the market square, and the butchers Cross, Leonard and Staples and Thomas Pyke the draper, Mr Morris with footwear and uncle Arthur Bradley the coalman who was the last to sell turf from our fen. Less welcomed until needed were the doctors Nicolle and Nickson and, for the stockbreeders, Albert Rouse the vet, but

The Steelyard, as it should read, used for weighing horse-drawn loads before weighbridges were introduced, remains as a relic in Fountain Lane. It has served no other purpose since Soham station opened in 1879. It escaped the fire that gutted 'The Fountain' commercial hotel on 4th May 1900. The sun-blind is protecting the delicacies in Clement Fuller's shop. *(Jane Hull Collection)*

Churchgate Street and the old Grammar School c. 1900.
(Jane Hull Collection)

Station Road, formerly Pump Lane c.1900.
(Jane Hull Collection)

A solemn occasion in 1921.
(Jane Hull Collection)

we boys were ever waiting for the presence of C.J.R. Fyson's threshing tackle between harvest and spring, the very name evoking the thrust of steam. We knew too that Soham Grammar School had been there since 1686 and that Soham could organize its celebrations as well as any town in the land.

Soham presented us with our social crescendo of the year on the third Sunday in June. This had gone on since the 1890s and Soham Hospital Sundays, once seen and heard, were never to be forgotten. Most villages had their Hospital Sundays from spring to autumn, raising essential funds before there was a National Health Service. Wicken's coincided, as did most, with the village feast, which was May 13th, and was exciting to us, but Soham's emptied the surrounding villages, persuaded the ladies to buy new hats and dresses while praying first and last for fine weather to preserve them. The scene was photographed from the same high vantage points year after year, thus compiling a catalogue of fashions until the onset of the second world war, with a cast of thousands, leaving those surrounding parishes in the care of the aged, the infirm and the very few who could resist this high point of summer.

From infancy I went with my mother and sister for the day, dining at great uncle Ted's in Brook Street, hopefully on the season's first new potatoes and redcurrant pie, and going on to Mill Corner and great aunt Mary's for tea who greeted us like flowers in the sun and laid on a banquet largely selected from the exquisite shelves of Clement Fuller. Aunt Mary knew we had to eat homemade food at home and she was a mischievous spoiler this once a year.

Then on to the great parade where I would want to lose my mother and sister as soon as possible to join up with my dad who would arrive on his bike and take me home on his crossbar afterwards. And there we are together, caught looking up at the camera in 1929, that shy man so held to hard work that he had no idea how to carry his hands when he was in such company, although I am commandeering one of them. The photographer's, Bolton of Ely and Shepherd of Soham did wonders for compilers of local history.

We would mingle for many a hesitant encounter and the day would live in our heads for weeks.

And what a turnout it was, as the photographs show! This was the order of the parade in 1932:

1 Soham Comrades Silver Prize Band
2 Soham British Legion
3 Fordham British Legion
4 Isleham and Mildenhall Bands
5 Soham and District Fire Brigades
6 Nurses' Hospital Van
7 Oddfellows' Club and Banner (Star of Charity Lodge)
8 Shepherds' Club (Providence Lodge L.A.D.S)
9 Star of Providence
10 United Brethren
11 Wicken Coronation Silver Band
12 Boys' Brigade and Life Boys
13 Anchor Slate Club Decorated Car
17 Salvation Army Band
18 Soham Motor Ambulance

It held us children spellbound. Nothing could stop us proclaiming our own band above the rest, but we knew well enough that Soham's, through the genius of Fred Talbot, who also instructed Wicken Band for their successful competitions later, was supreme. And those firemen under their flashing helmets, like centurions on the march, looked awesome, with their captain, Townsend, at the head of the column, drawing pride from every drumbeat, filling us with visions of brave rescues and tumbling walls. Tin boxes were crashed against our ears for the hospital fund, which would benefit hugely, and there was nothing we could want more at the summer solstice than this display of pomp and unity.

I travelled frequently on that crossbar to visit Desbois the ironmongers for cartridges, to Arthur Knight's for clothing and the

Soham Parade, 1908.
(Author's Collection)

Soham Parade, 1913.
(Author's Collection)

Soham Parade, 1928.
(Author's Collection)

1929. The author stands, hatless, in the foreground holding his father's hand.
(Author's Collection)

Soham Parade, 1931. *(Author's Collection)*

1932. Each year the photographs were displayed, people spotted themselves and their kin in the crowd and bought the prints for the home archives. This print, for instance, was borrowed from Tom Money of Wicken who is in the bottom left corner wearing a peaked cap, turning to look up at the camera. *(Author's Collection)*

Day and Knight exchange of greetings — or to Fred Hutt's for haircuts and a luxurious shave for father. As likely as not I would take in more than enough of Fred's cigarette smoke as he let the ash spill over my apron. Jack Fuller took some of the trade off him later. Those old names and firms have gone now and the shopfronts show less evidence of wellbeing.

In time the cinema, barred form us for a long time as a modern excess, became an acceptable form of entertainment for fast-growing children and then it was worth the sacrifice of twopence a week for parents to get us off their hands on a Saturday afternoon. For that was all it cost to attend the matinees at the Regal, the shell of which remains in Clay Street with not much less of its original red-brick splendour intact. Suddenly, it seemed, we boys were mobile together, some given new bikes, some hand-me-downs perhaps with blocks on the pedals and a piece of sacking for a saddle for legs shorter than the original owner's, setting off as a creaking armada thrilled at the prospect ahead, along the treeless, winding road where the telegraph poles hummed the tune of liberty and adventure.

It was no more than a converted barn, we were reminded, but it was, with the Central cinema in Fountain Lane, our palace of delights from then on. We could stack our bikes for nothing in Mr Rouse's yard then race in a pack to the box office where, should it appear necessary, we might have our boots or shoes inspected before being issued with a ticket. Then into the subfusc lighting and a saturation of 'June scent,' priming us for transportation into haunting skyscraper cities, the gambling halls of Monte Carlo or Shangri La itself; into the exercise yards of San Quentin or Singsing or for all the fun we could absorb from Eddie Cantor, the Hulberts or the Aldwych farceurs. Or, more reassuringly, into the hills and dusty plains of the wild West.

It was necessary to thump our way down to the front seats, there to be distanced by the local boys who excluded us from their bonhomie. When this first happened we were afraid of having our hard-won twopennyworth spoiled, but once the lights dimmed further and the beams flashed overhead and the curtains scraped

Soham Flower Show, 1908.
(Cambridgeshire Collection)

Billy Sennitt (left) and Jacko Bullman (extreme right) competing at Isleham Sports in the 1930s.
(Author's Collection)

apart to reveal the censor's certificate they swivelled to the front on a muffled tattoo of behinds, roared their delight and sat still. Then it was lift-off to the beating chords of Warner, the drumming searchlights of Twentieth Century Fox, the sparking torch of Columbia or the momentous morse pips of RKO Radio and all the noise was an expression of pleasure. We got in behind Tom Mix, Buck Jones, Ken Maynard, Tim McCoy, Tom Tyler, Hoot Gibson or John Wayne and were as loud as the locals in our support. Inhibited country lads, we could let off steam unashamedly in there and not be individually identified and on that trail home we would be shooting from the hip and changing our speech to match.

Perhaps it never seemed that far from Soham to the Wild West, what with those rustic environs, those wild-haired ponies and steers and geese in farmyards and on those coral-commons, while even that little station seemed a likely place to sort good from evil at sundown. Came the age of real-life sexual attraction, when we were all working and spurning the matinees to turn out on Saturday and Sunday nights, keeping in secure groups while hoping to mingle with the girls. They were the awkward, poignant times of growing up, walking endlessly up and down the long street with no more success than flippant encounters. I got on well with those Soham girls — until one of them turned my head. Others older did the same, the landworkers incongruous in navy blue suits, tight collars, porkpie hats and patent shoes, still treading clods along the pavements. Many would soon enter the pubs then feast on fish, chips and peas at Garner's in the market square or Carter's on the corner of Station Road and bike home in groups.

Other events pulled us to Soham. While we were anticipating the fair coming to our village feast we would also be gazing from our bedroom windows across the dark mere hoping to see stars sparkling near the ground. This would be Soham fair under way and since we were barred from it we would want to know all about it from those who had been because it might well come on to us. Then again, it might not, for ours sometimes came in from the other direction from some fabulous global resource of fairs and whilst having our eyes fixed on study in school we would be awaiting the shudder from the approaching engine and its column of wheels and ponies and would be itching to charge down the street to get there first.

Walter Redit in 1932. (Author's Collection)

Soham Flower Show and Sports in August was generally open to us — and certainly from 1934 when our Wicken boxer of fond memory, Walter Redit, the future lightweight champion of the Eastern Area, made his debut there in opposition to Soham's Jackie Bishop and our home-grown racing cyclists, Billy Sennitt and Jacko Bullman, both of whom were to settle in Soham, were sweeping up the prize money there and elsewhere.

Changes to this pattern of life seemed unlikely then, but the war pointed us all, suddenly, in another direction. Soham today has its Carnival in place of the Hospital Sunday and it has revived its Flower Show and Sports and has a Pumpkin Fair. The town looks much the same as it did but the farmsteads have reduced. Soham has an excellent Sports Centre and has been bypassed to some advantage, but its tradesmen have much to complain about since the installation of traffic calming measures that keep people away and seriously restrict emergency services that can become a matter of life and death.

Soham, then, today is not the same; but you can say that of any town or village after half a century of accelerated change. It is much bigger, but the old native friendliness and ways of speech still persist to remind you of an era when its people could keep up to date while depending on continuity and security at home.

2. THE SAVING OF SOHAM

The summer had been warm and dry in Britain and its people after, nearly five years of war, were waiting for D-Day — the beginning of the end. All knew the landings in Europe were imminent and that the first list of casualties would follow all too soon. It was no time for crises on the home front to claim the front pages — and they seldom did with so much coming from the theatres of war, good or bad. The threats from the air had extended to doodlebugs, chugging over like motorcycles with flaming tails until they cut out to blast holes anywhere, and V-2 rockets diving on London, leaving huge craters and many casualties. The crisis that occurred in the small hours of Friday June 2nd 1944 in 'a market town in Cambridgeshire' could claim but passing interest in the national press at this time.

Not so for the people of Soham, that market town disguised at a time of geographical censorship, although they were soon to be reassured that but for acts of courage and self-sacrifice outstanding even in wartime their troubles would have been far worse.

London, on the very day of the Soham incident, was appointed the World's News Centre when the allied forces invaded and it was reported too that the United States Air Force had dropped 63,000 tons of bombs on Germany, the occupied countries and The Balkans in May and was stepping up the intensity all the time. On the previous Tuesday, May 30th, the American Cemetery at Madingley near Cambridge was dedicated with due ceremony and all knew there were many more spaces to be filled there before the war was over.

Like most of my generation I was in uniform and while not far away it was some time before I knew the precise location of the Soham incident. In the meantime I might not have been unduly held by such headlines as 'THREE MEN SAVE A TOWN,' 'HE DIED LIKE A SOLDIER TO SAVE AN ENGLISH VILLAGE' and 'HERO SAVED TOWN FROM DISASTER.' I might have guessed sooner from the indecision of the national press on whether Soham was a town or a village! It was a long time after, following

Soham station in 1939. The tall figure of Frank Bridges stands against the stationmaster's house.
(Cambridgeshire Collection)

two years abroad, when the full story of that grim night was put before me, a story summarised many times since with freedom of interpretation, but which I now unfold from the beginning.

On May 31st 1944 a consignment of bombs and components for the United States Air Force was taken off ship and on to sixty-one railway wagons at Immingham on the Humber, destined for White Colne in Essex. This long train left Immingham Sidings at 2.55 a.m. On June 1st, travelling so slowly that it took seven hours to cover the eighty-nine miles to March in Cambridgeshire. It arrived at March Yard, which was subsiduary to the nearby marshalling yard at Whitemoor (where today stands the high security prison), where the wagons were, as always, carefully inspected. The ten leading wagons were then detached to be worked forward by convenient services later, leaving the fifty-one wagons and the guard's van in Number One Siding Coal Yard. These remained in the yard for fourteen-and-a-half hours unaltered in formation until they left at 12.15 a.m. On Friday June 2nd as the delayed 11.40 p.m. (June 1st) train from Whitemoor to White Colne.

Forty-four of those wagons were laden with 250-pound and 500-pound bombs, unfused, amounting to approximately four hundred tons in all and another six with detonators and primers, fuses, wire release gear and bomb tail fins, all firmly stacked under tarpaulin sheets of low combustibility with the care that had prevented any major crisis in the transportation of weaponry on British railways throughout the war. One wagon remained empty.

This train was about 390 yards long and there were no gradients between March and Soham to unsettle such loads. For the four-and-three-quarter miles from Ely Dock Junction to Soham the line was, and is, single, while from Soham it was, and remains, double. The train stopped at Ely twice where observers saw nothing unusual aboard. All the Soham signals were clear for the train's approach when it was moving at between fifteen and twenty miles per hour with the engine steaming lightly along the level line. Then, a few yards beyond the Up signal, the driver, Benjamin Gimbert, noticed some steam issuing from the left-hand injector and looked out of his cab window. Although he could see but nine to twelve inches into the left-hand rear corner of the first wagon above the rear of his tender Ben saw flames rising some eighteen inches form the bottom.

The flames were spreading rapidly as if taking hold, unaccountably, of inflammable material. He sounded his whistle to alert the guard and stopped the train gently, taking about three minutes, for any jolt could have proved disastrous. Having stopped some ninety yards short of the station platform ramps he urged his fireman, James Nightall, to get down to uncouple the burning wagon from the rest, advising him to take a coal hammer in case the coupling was already too hot to handle. Jim leapt to the task, released the coupling and climbed back on the footplate within a minute and Ben sped the engine and its fireball away, aiming to get it into the open country. 140 yards forward into the station, now illuminated by the burning wagon, he slowed down to shout to the signalman, Frank 'Sailor' Bridges: 'Sailor — have you anything between here and Fordham! Where's the mail!' But Frank was ahead of him, having not received the mail train and having requested another engine to tow the detached wagons away. Ben had crossed to the fireman's side to talk to Frank who was waiting on that offside platform with a full fire bucket hoping, forlornly, to douse the flames, putting his life at risk like the others to avert disaster.

He had no moment to answer or act. The earth shattered in one enormous blast, smashing him to the floor mortally wounded. Less than seven minutes had elapsed since Ben saw the fire. At approximately 1.43 a.m. Forty-four general purpose bombs each weighing five hundred pounds, in total containing 5.14 tons of explosive content, went up as one, reducing the station to rubble, killing Jim Nightall outright, blasting Ben Gimbert some two hundred yards away.

The first miracle of this night was the courage these railwaymen found to face such responsibilities, the second was the survival of Ben Gimbert to tell the tale. He landed on grass near the Station Hotel and crawled his way to the doorstep of Horace Taylor's shop at the bottom of Station Road. He was then found by Railway

Ganger Reed staggering about wanting to know if his mates and the rest of the train were safe. Jim's fate was not know at that moment but Ben at first refused to go to hospital until he knew. Red Cross women were in charge of the ambulance when it came and to spare them Ben, who weighted eighteen-and-a-half stones, refused to be carried on or off. Critically injured, he was kept in ignorance of Jim's death until an innocent visitor to his hospital bedside offered his condolences and thus set back the big man's recovery quite a bit.

There was a fourth hero in Herbert Clarke of Ipswich, the guard, who had suspected problems when the train slackened speed when his van was a train's length away from the distant signal. He saw the fire in the front wagon and helped his driver slow down with a light application of his van brake. When stationary the train is the responsibility of the guard and Herbert, recognizing the intention of Jim Nightall, got down and rushed forward to help him. The engine and its leading wagon moved away as he was still going forward. Then the blast hurled him back along the track some eighty feet and left him concussed. He gradually recovered enough to re-light the extinguished van lamps and then he walked back dazedly to the front of the train to ascertain the damage. Herbert was 59 and in deep shock but he gathered detonators to put down on the rails along the two-and-a-quarter miles back to Barway Junction, arriving at about 3.30 a.m. utterly spent, where he was helped into the box by Signalman Cyril King. Herbert was not to know Frank Bridges had got his messages through before the blast destroyed all communications.

Indeed, judging by his quick reactions, Frank may have seen the fire before Ben, for he had aroused Sub-Ganger Will Fuller, who was living in Mount Pleasant Cottage a hundred yards from the station, soon enough to enable Fuller to notice the fire the moment the train pulled up about 230 yards away. Fuller was then pulling on his clothes by the bedroom window as he heard the uncoupling, then he saw the burning wagon moving forward until it was obscured by the station buildings. In moments the explosion shattered Fuller's cottage and buried him and his wife and daughter in the debris. It was Fuller later who gave evidence of seeing blue flames among the yellow rising from the wagon and of detecting a smell like burning gas. The possibility of this deriving from the residue of the wagon's previous load of bulk sulphur was studied at the inquiry.

It even seemed possible that Frank Bridges had been notified of the fire in the wagon by the Barway signalman, Cyril King, but King later avowed he saw nothing to disturb him on the train, saw no sparks coming from the engine and caught no smell of burning beyond the normal as the train slowly passed his signal box at about 1.31 a.m. He saw one of the engine men exchange tokens using the lineside apparatus, watched the tail light of the train moving away and signalled 'Train out of junction' back to Ely Dock Junction. When the train was about three-quarters-of-a-mile away he saw a pink glow that he took to come from the firebox, then saw the train obscured by the bend and soon after heard the explosion.

Five others followed Ben and Frank to hospital with severe injuries including the station master, Harry Oliver, who had been found pinned under his bed badly concussed after the house had tumbled about him and his wife, his nineteen-year-old daughter Pat and his ten-year-old son Dick, who escaped with minor injuries. Mrs Oliver wandered away seeking shelter and was taken in, but there was no room for her daughter who had to go elsewhere. Mrs Oliver suffered from shattered nerves for a long time after this night.

The streets of Soham were littered with glass, shop goods were blown into the streets and the station was replaced by a crater fifteen feet deep and sixty-six feet across. Only a buffer and a socket casting were left of the wagon, the rest being driven downwards, there to stay so that the lines could be restored quickly at that time of acute national emergency. The tender was a twisted mass still attached to the engine which was wholly derailed yet received no serious structural damage other than to the cab, its light platework, boiler and cylinder lagging. The larger part of the train disconnected by Jim Nightall, lethal in its content, was hit by no worse than minor splinters and thus the town of Soham was saved from utter destruction by human courage beyond praise. So many of those who recalled the night for me would have been killed or badly maimed but for the self-sacrifice of those men.

Hardly had the light from the burning truck and the explosion extinguished themselves than they were replaced by flames from the nearby gas holders, eerily dancing over the scene of destruction. The huge advantage thereafter was having so many trained units at hand to deal with every problem. The Wardens and Home Guard were swiftly there tending the injured and comforting the rest and it was they who summoned the other services needed, all of them on wartime alert. It was a clear but moonless night but luckily the electricity and water supplies were not affected and these were soon vital to the work in hand. The National Fire Service soon put out the fire at the gas works and they were soon joined by the Local Rescue and Ambulance Party reinforced by Royal Air Force ambulances, by Isleham Ambulance Party, Burwell Rescue Party, Fordham Red Cross Ambulance and Royal Air Force personnel from Snailwell and Newmarket.

Once the seriously injured were away to hospital the minor cases were taken to an Emergency Rest Centre set up in the Grammar School, supervised by the Women's Voluntary Services who worked in shifts throughout the weekend, closing down to allow the school to resume on the Monday. Damage had been done to the official Local First Aid Point, but the nurses were able to treat several cases there. The local police sergeant set up an Incident Post in one room of Roselyn, the Bradleys' cottage in Mereside, the church hall was used by the YMCA for serving tea and a mobile canteen arrived from Cambridge to sustain all who need more than tea throughout a traumatic night. The Queen's Messengers; Flying Squad also brought in cooked food and supplies in large containers from the emergency depot in Over. At the Rest Centre there was also an Information Bureau using a travelling van with a loudspeaker and clothes were brought in form Cambridge and parcels from the Lord Mayor of London's Distress Fund arrived during the following week and were distributed in the Baptist schoolroom by the Rotary Club and representatives of the 'Daily Sketch..' The British Red

The Aftermath.
(Cambridgeshire Collection; W. Martin Lane)

Cross also treated many minor injuries and the two local doctors were kept busy all night and for days afterwards catching up with minor injuries that might have turned worse.

Gradually the chaos of that night gave way to the relative order of day, unravelling the extent of the damage and the miracle of Ben Gimbert's escape from the epicentre of the blast. Houses and shops as far away as the high street and to the north of the town in Julius Martin Lane and south to Stone Bridge had roofs, walls, ceilings and windows shattered. On the same day as the blast the Wardens took a census of the damaged buildings, as a result of which about a hundred workmen were brought into Soham to speed up repairs and many homes were repaired by evening. It was estimated there had been damage to 761 properties in all, 13 of them beyond repair,

The Crater.
(Cambridgeshire Collection; W. Martin Lane)

153 seriously damaged of which 36 were rendered temporarily uninhabitable, these within 350 yards and the rest within 900 yards of the explosion. The church, only 700 yards away, suffered only damage to glass. Windows were shattered in Wicken and Fordham.

Fourteen public authorities gave assistance to Soham, bypassing red tape with admirable enterprise at a time when emergency plans were constantly being implemented. Many vehicles were made available to transport the homeless to friends and temporary homes and very quickly too at such a time the Army Police set up a guard on the district. Nothing was left to chance. Rationing had kept people low in stocks of food, although hoarding had been an early symptom of the war. Emergency ration cards were provided, entitling the holders to a week's supply of food and clothing coupons and

The Stricken Leviathan.
(Cambridgeshire Collection; W. Martin Lane)

The shifting of the engine. If Frank Bridges had run from the scene behind his signal box he would have survived. *(Cambridgeshire Collection; W. Martin Lane)*

(Cambridgeshire Collection; W. Martin Lane)

(Cambridgeshire Collection; W. Martin Lane)

Filling the crater.
(Cambridgeshire Collection; W. Martin Lane)

(Cambridgeshire Collection; 'News Chronicle')

Will Fuller's cottage after the explosion. Will was in hospital while others were retrieving belongings. The cottage, 'Mount Pleasant,' was, remarkably, restored and is lived in today.

grants of money were issued for crisis needs. Even a mobile laundry van arrived to wash what was taken to it and the dignitaries to arrive included the Bishop of Ely and the Regional Commissioner and other top personnel of Civil Defence Control from Cambridge and Newmarket. The country was geared for worse than this night at this and earlier stages of the war.

My kin, the Bradleys, living in Roselyn cottage near the Station Hotel, who were bombed awake like the rest, found themselves uninjured but the house damaged. The roof facing the station had lost its slates but it was the rebound, caused by a vacuum from the explosion, that hit them harder, forcing in the windows on the other side and a bedroom door off its hinges, wedging it firmly in the door frame. Eva Bradley, the mother, rushed at once to her baby John lying in his cot, flinging herself over him but finding him unharmed. When she returned to her bed she found three bricks lying where her head would have been. She thought later of her china cabinet and its precious treasurers, but although the locked door had been forced open and shut and although they removed rubble and dust, not one item of china or glass had been broken! The Bradleys moved into an empty cottage next door while theirs was being repaired.

Not far from the station stands Clark and Butcher's Mill, then in overtime production for the war effort, but only its steam engine had been damaged in the explosion. The mill's Managing Director, Jack Clark, recorded his impressions of that night in 'A Master Miller Remembers' in the 1970s. Shocked awake in the adjacent Mill House, he trod broken glass to the smashed window only to be stabbed in the face by a broken curtain rail. The mill was his responsibility, but in the road he was soon distracted by people wandering about dazed and dusty as if after an earthquake. Many had no idea what had happened or what to do or where to go, so he led some back to his house where his wife, a native of Wicken, made tea for them, boiling the kettle on an open fire since gas supplies had been cut off for both Soham and Fordham. Mr Clark was also a special constable and a member of the Home Guard.

A Londoner living nearby, Mrs E. Tyrell, said the night was worse

Clarke and Butcher's Mill between the wars.
(Jane Hull Collection)

than any she had suffered in the blitz and her neighbour, Mr Wallace, an ex-naval man, likened the blast to the force of a typhoon. Another nearby resident, Mr J.T. Skipper, pulled his three-year-old grandson to safety as part of the roof of their cottage was crashing down on his bed, the boy escaping with no worse than a scratch. The flames from the gas works were unnerving while they lasted and the Maltons, living in numbers one and two Gas Lane, were relieved to see them put out. The blast had damaged their cottages but left them uninjured, the only casualty being the family canary which succumbed to gas fumes. Two chunks of the station platform landed in the garden of number two, now called 'The Maltons,' where lives Edith Canham, nee Malton, and husband Stuart, formerly of Wicken, and there the chunks remain as weighty ornaments.

There are light-hearted recollections of the night. John Gilbey, then aged five, of Bushel Lane on the other side of Soham, recalls waking up and wondering at the strange whirring sound downstairs. The family gramophone, long seized up, had been freed by the blast, but once it had would down it would not wind up again. John Ford, the Biology and Chemistry Master and Deputy Headmaster at the Grammar School awoke in the belief, life many another, that this was a bombing from the air, inexplicably without siren warning. As ARP Post Warden he pulled his trousers over his pyjamas and cycled down Clay Street over glass — without getting a puncture — and joined the helpers. For a few days he was apt to be known as 'Bluey' for the colour of those pyjamas showing below his trousers. There had to be moments to ease the strain.

Eric Isaacson, a Soham butcher and, at 24, a Leading Fireman in the National Fire Service, received directions soon after the blast to go to the blazing gas works then to the Goods Yard, which received some damage, to attend a small fire there. When an American officer asked him if he had seen the fireman Eric directed him to the gas works, not realising he meant the engine fireman. Corrected, he accompanied that officer to the crater and got down into it with him. An ambulance backed to the crater using a small searchlight which soon exposed the body of Jim Nightall. As the smallest of the

Firemen at the scenes. Behind are Bill Shaw and James Butler the messenger; front are, left, Arthur Ely who for a time kept the 'Black Horse' public house at Wicken, Eric Isaacson and Joe West.
(Eric Isaacson Collection)

An earlier task for the firemen and others. Four 500-lb bombs dropped behind Britten's Garage, Town's End, Soham, in 1942 — without exploding. Eric Isaacson kneels by the crater. *(Eric Isaacson Collection)*

Up comes one of the bombs, defused and safe.
(Eric Isaacson Collection)

four men now in the crater Eric was persuaded to release the body from the rubble near those huge driving wheels and the hissing locomotive and the searing heat of the firebox,. He found Jim with his head resting on an arm as if in sleep. His shirt was open baring his chest where scalding has peeled the skin. He turned the twisted body so that the others could pull it out, then he crawled his way out from the worst ordeal of his life.

There was still some fear at this stage that the bombs on the other wagons might go up and Eric was one of those ordered to inspect them, adding danger upon danger to one who was fast asleep not long before. It would have occurred to no-one on that night that locomotive W.D. 7337 of the 2-8-0 'British Austerity' heavy goods type weighing 128 tons with tender, lying there stricken, would come to be rebuilt. Yet it was. Originally built by the North British Locomotive Company of Glasgow as works number 25205 in 1943, it ran after refurbishment for many years on the Longmoor Military Railway in Hampshire as 'Sir Guy Williams' and was finally retired and scrapped in 1967.

The Soham line was vital for carrying heavy freight at this time and it had to be restored as soon as possible. To this end the Cambridge breakdown crane arrived in Soham at 5.10 a.m. to re-rail the engine and remove the wreckage of the tender. Through Lieutenant-Colonel C.P. Parker of the Royal Engineers the Railway Company acquired the assistance of about a hundred United States engineer troops with two bulldozers to fill the crater and firm the surface to carry new rails where 120 feet had been destroyed. This party arrived at 10.50 a.m. about an hour-and-a-half after the arrival of the Company's ballast train and they worked throughout the day. The two lines through the station were reopened to traffic at 8.20 p.m. after a lapse of only eighteen-and-a-half hours. The station, as such, was opened for light passenger traffic next day, June 3rd, with temporary booking facilities, but emergency signalling had to remain for a further four days.

The Inquiry into the accident was opened on 16th June headed by Major G.R.S. Wilson for the Ministry of War Transport, assisted by Captain N. Fawcett the Inspector of Explosives at the War Office. Ben Gimbert was the chief witness, supported by Herbert Clarke and Will Fuller, but none of them was fit to give evidence until 18th July, although Ben was interviewed briefly on 5th June. The first suspicion was that an over-heated axlebox had caused the fire but every possibility was studied and nobody was certain at the end.

The Carriage and Wagon Examiner at March, G. Stevens, a man of long experience, had taken an hour to examine the train there, feeling all the axleboxes after the eighty-nine mile journey with the back of his hand, tapping all the wheels and looking round and under every wagon. Such men were always alert for hazards, not to mention sabotage, at that time, and were taking no chances. Stevens found no defects and no axlebox likely to overheat to cause a fire and none of the wagons was overdue for oiling. He and two other examiners had seen overheated axleboxes but had never known one to start a fire. The War Office and the Railway Police probed for long into the possibilities of sabotage without finding any reason to believe this was the cause. An attempt to ignite one of the wagon sheets by using combustible material and simulated draught such as would fan flames on a moving train also failed to convince and Major Wilson was forced finally to summarize thus: 'I think it must be assumed that there was some substance present in the wagon which was particularly sensitive to ignition by a trifling spark from the train engine (or perhaps from the engine of a passing train) which otherwise would have proved harmless.' Nothing had come of trying to set light to a dusting of sulphur residue such as might have been clinging to the wagon and the Inquiry's conclusion must be said to have been inconclusive.

A 'Salute the Soldier' service had been planned for Soham church on the following Sunday, to include a parade in the Recreation Ground, but this was altered to a service of thanksgiving for the saving of Soham. The church needless to say, was packed. Tiny fragments of glass were still tinkling down from the windows as the Reverend Percy Fletcher Boughey began his address with the wholly appropriate words: 'But for such men as these . . .' There were big attendances too at the funerals of Jim Nightall and Frank Bridges on 6th June when donations to the Tribute and Relief Fund amounted to £1,760. This money was, however, distributed thinly rather than given to those who most needed it. Those funerals coincided, of course, with D-Day and all minds were soon turned to that.

The youngest person living in Soham on the night of the explosion was six days old. She was Diane, daughter of Gladys and Roger Turner, living so near at Mill Corner where the ceiling spilled dust over the bed without causing more damage to the occupants than leaving a piece of grit in the baby's eye. Her life was saved by brave men that night. Jim Brown had been the first Soham man to be called up for active service and when he and the other survivors came home for good it was, through the intervention of those

Troops already prepared for the 'Salute the Soldier Week' service arrive for the service of thanksgiving . *(Cambridgeshire Collection)*

The great moment of solemnity and relief, Sunday June 4th 1944. (Cambridgeshire Collection)

railwaymen, to the town he had left behind.

The awards of the George Cross to Ben Gimbert and Jim Nightall were gazetted on July 25th 1944, the only instance of the award being made to two railwaymen for the same incident. The implication that Frank Bridges may not have been aware of the contents of the wagons when he came forward to assist must be dismissed, if only because if he had not known he would have anticipated the worst at such a time. Although drivers and firemen and others involved along the routes were given no specific details of the loads they were pulling or controlling they were seldom in any doubt during the war. The guard was fully aware since it was his responsibility to inspect the wagons and the signalmen along the routes were sharp on recognition. But with awards it appeared to be all or nothing and neither he nor Herbert Clarke received any acknowledgement of their deeds apart from being included in the inscriptions on the plaques placed in Soham church and, eventually, Soham Village College.

The presence of combustible material on that front wagon will remain a mystery, but it certainly fueled suspicions of sabotage. That sparks from railway engines could cause fires was known to all of us old enough to recall the burnt patches alongside the tracks. With such a possibility I am left wondering why the front wagon was loaded with bombs and not harmless components, particularly since the second wagon was left empty. However, official speculation ended in 1944 and we are left to honour the heroes of fifty years ago.

We should honour too the conscience and concern of the Americans present in this area at the time for the people of Soham after their shattering experience. The American Red Cross were soon distributing parcels, wonderfully varied in their contents at such a time of austerity, to all the infants in Soham. There never was such an interchange of sympathy and unity of purpose.

Buckingham Palace, Tuesday 10th October 1944. (Left to right), Joyce, Peggy, Ben and Violet Gimbert.
(Joyce Dedman Collection)

3. THE SAVIOURS OF SOHAM

BENJAMIN GIMBERT G.C. (1903 — 1976)

He was born on February 6th 1903 in Ely, the sixth child of Florence Mary and George William Gimbert, a farm worker, who were to have sixteen children in all. The family were shortly to move to Sutton-in-the Isle and of those children only one, Mrs J. Edgerley of Chatteris, is living today.

Ben was a bright schoolboy who showed the beginnings of a mathematical mind during his short time at Sutton school, but he was forced to leave at the age of eleven to work on the land. He withstood this job for four years, until 1918, and then with parental encouragement he moved to live with an aunt in Peterborough hoping for a job on the railways. Ben's childhood longing to become an engine driver had translated into genuine ambition and he was happy to start work for what was then the Great Eastern Railway at Peterborough as a call-boy. He then became an engine cleaner, moving into lodgings in March, and then, in 1921, a fireman.

On October 25th 1926 he married Violet, daughter of Charlotte and William Bradshaw, a railway guard, who were to have a house built in Estover Road, March, with half an acre of land from which they could supplement their income by growing shrubs and vegetables. Here, at number 81, they also took in lodgers. Ben and Violet were to have three children. The firstborn, Joyce, soon had to move in with her grandparents while a house was being built, this time at number 7 Estover Road, by the Railway Board, an up-to-date home with bathroom, hot water and three bedrooms. Ben took out a mortgage to buy this house and worked intensely hard to do so, doing double trips and keeping long hours to keep up the payments.

Thirteen months after the birth of Joyce a second daughter, Peggy, was born and life ran smoothly for the family.

Ben Gimbert grew into a huge man weighing eighteen-and-a-half stones and reaching six feet, one inch in height. He was as easy-

Ben Gimbert as a teenager.
(Joyce Dedman Collection)

Violet Bradshaw as a teenager.
(Joyce Dedman Collection)

Ben and Violet on a happy day at Hunstanton, c. 1925.
(Joyce Dedman Collection)

October 26th 1926, Ben and Violet's wedding day. *(Joyce Dedman Collection)*

Violet and Ben with Joyce, their firstborn in 1927. (Joyce Dedman Collection)

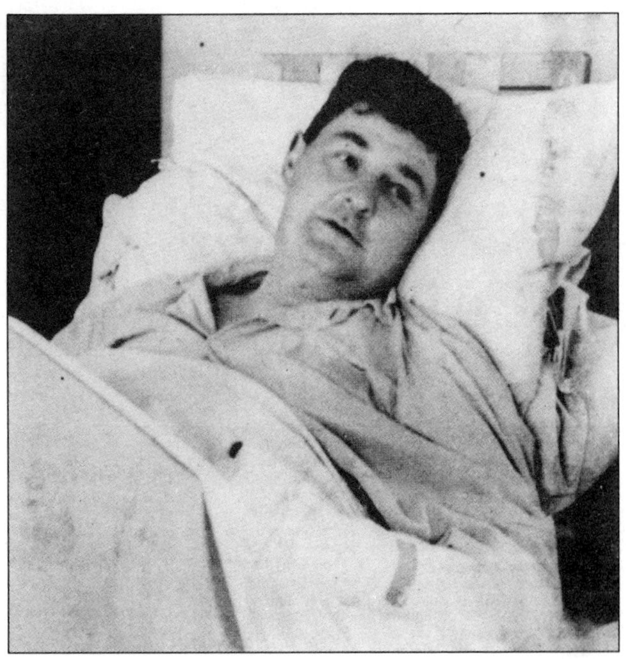

Ben recovering in Newmarket Hospital, June 1944.

Ben wears his medals proudly after the war.

going and popular as they come, settled within the railway fraternity based in March, loving his leisure hours playing cards, dominoes or billiards at his local Conservative Club of which he was a proud member while remaining loyal to his union, ASLEF. His cherished ambition was to become an engine driver and he studied hard towards this, bringing into his home others who wanted to find the right atmosphere for their own studies. One of these was a tall, lean, pale, silent young man called Jim Nightall who made little impression on Joyce, who had then grown into an attractive teenager working at the local Regent Cinema, perhaps with heightened ideals about young men. Jim was then in lodgings in March with a Mr F.C. Doncaster.

Ben realised his ambition to become an engine driver in 1938, after which, as acting driver, he had to wait for an engine vacancy. The family then entered a tragic phase in their lives. A still-born son preceded the birth of Michael in 1942, but he died eleven-and-a-half months later, leaving the family distraught. Losing his son and heir cast a blight over Ben's acquisition of his first engine in 1943, but he had dependable Jim Nightall beside him as fireman and the two became fast friends.

While still mourning the loss of Michael the mother and two girls received the news from Soham. Ben had been driving but two years and now he was expected to die of his injuries. Hopes for his recovery were indeed thin after he was taken into White Lodge Hospital, Newmarket. Thirty-two pieces of shrapnel and glass had entered his body, his lungs and eardrums were damaged and delayed shock was expected to do for the big man. Violet rushed to Newmarket and took lodgings to be at his side, with little hope of remaining there for six weeks. Yet within a few days Ben was declared stable and relatively comfortable, even able to give a brief account of the events leading up to the explosion. He remained in disbelief that he should have survived while two others died.

When released he had to return to hospital frequently for further treatment and was never the same man. Then came the commendations and honours, inducing a sense of guilt that he was the only one alive to receive them. While lying there in hospital he learned that he and Jim, posthumously, had been awarded the George Cross (dated 25th July 1944) and the London and North Easter Railway Company's Silver Medal for Courage and Resource (dated 2nd June 1944). There followed the Daily Herald Order of Industrial Heroism Medal (dated 26th November 1944) and after being invited with his family to attend the Coronation of 1953 Ben was awarded the Coronation Medal to make up the quartet.

Once on his feet Ben soon overcame his handicaps of a damaged arm and useless finger, bronchial trouble and partial deafness enough to apply for a return to work. His employers sympathetically offered him office work but he turned this down firmly. He wanted to get back on the footplate and they conceded, but he remained a shunting driver off the main lines. Yet no sooner had he returned to work than Ben was reminded he had to pay back the compensation money he had received! He was not able to put in extra hours to make up for this but was confined to shifts from either 6 a.m. to 2 p.m. or 2 p.m. to 10 p.m.

Meanwhile he had to get used to the role of a celebrity, his best suit at the ready. The big occasion was the Investiture at Buckingham Palace on 10th October 1944 with Violet, Joyce and Peggy in proud attendance but on hearing of the necessity for this Ben asked wryly: 'Can't they put it through the letter box?' He was to attend several Royal Garden Parties and went to receptions at Windsor Castle, Hampton Court and the Mansion House meeting members of the Royal Family and there were those gatherings at the Cafe Royal every two years for holders of the Victoria and George Crosses. While easier among his mates, Ben began to spend more time at home than of yore but he remained the same solid friendly man they had always known.

In 1966 he suffered a heart attack and retired form the railway two years earlier than intended. He was further reduced by strokes later but continued to be feted. He attended his last VC and GC Reunion at the Cafe Royal in May 1976. While his son-in-law, Roland Dedman, went to order a taxi for their departure, Ben stood

CENTRAL CHANCERY OF THE ORDERS OF KNIGHTHOOD,

ST JAMES'S PALACE, S.W.1.

25th September 1944

CONFIDENTIAL.

Sir,

The King will hold an Investiture at Buckingham Palace on Tuesday, the 10th October, 1944, at which your attendance is requested.

It is requested that you should be at the Palace not later than 10.15 o'clock a.m.

DRESS–Service Dress, Morning Dress, Civil Defence Uniform or Dark Lounge Suit.

This letter should be produced on entering the Palace, as no further card of admission will be issued.

Two tickets for relations or friends to witness the Investiture may be obtained on application to this Office and you are requested to state your requirements on the form enclosed.

Please complete the enclosed form and return immediately to the Secretary, Central Chancery of the Orders of Knighthood, St. James's Palace, London, S.W.1.

I am, Sir,

Your obedient Servant,

Secretary.

Benjamin Gimbert, Esq.,
G.C.

3316

BUCKINGHAM PALACE.

Admit one to witness the

Investiture

(at 10.15 o'clock a.m.)

CENTRAL CHANCERY OF THE ORDERS OF KNIGHTHOOD

10 OCT 1944

Clarendon

Lord Chamberlain.

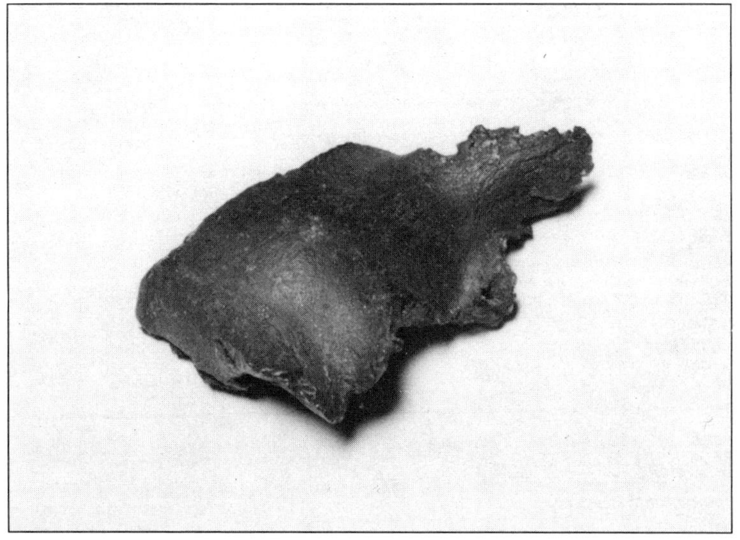

The biggest piece of shrapnel to have entered Ben's body, shown actual size. Smaller pieces were coming out of his body for the rest of his life.

1

The Lord Chamberlain is
commanded by Their Majesties to invite
Mr and Mrs Benjamin Gimbert
and the Misses Joyce & Peggy Gimbert
to an Afternoon Party in the Garden of Buckingham Palace,
on Thursday, 10th July, 1947, from 4 to 6 o'clock.
(Weather Permitting).

Morning Dress or Lounge Suit.
(Officers Service Dress).

F.10.

In York for the presentations of the LNER medal to Ben and Alice Nightall on behalf of her son in 1944. Left to right, the Area Manager for LNER, Mr Rees, Ben and Violet Gimbert, Charles Barber and his sister Alice and Jim Nightall's girl friend, Edna Belson. *(Joyce Dedman Collection)*

Ben back on the footplate but off the main lines after the war.
(Joyce Dedman Collection)

A Royal greeting for Ben in 1972, Sir John Smythe, right.
(Joyce Dedman Collection)

Ben's last portrait, taken two weeks before he died.
(Joyce Dedman Collection)

talking to the Duke of Edinburgh. Two weeks later Ben Gimbert died aged 73. He was buried in Eastwood Cemetery, March. He and Violet had been looking forward to celebrating their golden wedding anniversary for which their daughter Joyce had already made a cake.

Once her husband had died Violet had only her retirement pension to sustain her. The two pounds a week that came with the George Cross had ceased. She was 74 and independently minded enough to refuse help from her family. Soon the house at Estover Road became too big for her to manage and when it needed extensive repairs she decided to put it on the market. The property market had slumped at this time and it was a long time selling and when it did sell the amount she received was not enough to enable her to buy the warm modern flat she needed. All she owned of value otherwise was her husband's medals, locked away in a bank vault. She decided to sell them and they sold at Sotheby's for £7,000 in total. Luckily they were purchased by a philanthropical London businessman, Christopher Clayton, who offered them on permanent loan to March Museum. The museum reopened after refurbishment on April 17th 1985, displaying the medals for the first time. Violet Gimbert died on May 3rd 1991.

The new Soham *(Author's photograph)*

JAMES WILLIAM NIGHTALL G.C. (1922 — 1944)

He was born on 20th May 1922 at Croft River Side, Littleport, the only child of Alice Susan, nee Barber, and Walter Nightall a farm worker. Leaving school at fourteen he began working for Jim Kerridge, a local chicken farmer. He soon found this job unsatisfying and, like Ben Gimbert, he set his mind on joining the railways. He was taken on as a cleaner with the Locomotive Department of the London and North Eastern Railway at March where he moved into lodgings with Mr F.C. Doncaster.

THIS TABLET COMMEMORATES THE HEROIC ACTION OF FIREMAN J.W. NIGHTALL, G.C. WHO LOST HIS LIFE, & DRIVER B. GIMBERT, G.C. WHO WAS BADLY INJURED WHILST DETACHING A BLAZING WAGON FROM AN AMMUNITION TRAIN AT THIS STATION AT 1-43 A.M. ON JUNE 2ND 1944. THE STATION WAS TOTALLY DESTROYED AND CONSIDERABLE DAMAGE DONE BY THE EXPLOSION. THE DEVOTION TO DUTY OF THESE BRAVE MEN SAVED THE TOWN OF SOHAM FROM GRAVE DESTRUCTION. SIGNALMAN F. BRIDGES WAS KILLED WHILST ON DUTY & GUARD H. CLARKE SUFFERED FROM SHOCK.

"BE STRONG AND QUIT YOURSELVES LIKE MEN"

From the tablet in Soham Village College. After the death of Alice his wife Walter Nightall gave Jim's medal to the college.
(Ron Barber Collection)

Jim Nightall, right was a quiet young man but never without a friend. (Ron Barber Collection)

Summer blooms around the young man who was soon to die a hero's death. (Ron Barber Collection)

Jim Nightall applied himself so diligently that he advanced very quickly to the position of fireman and with the safety factor always to be considered such promotions were not offered lightly. Then came the outbreak of the second world war and the moment he was old enough Jim volunteered for the army. To his chagrin he was sent back to concentrate on his reserved occupation which sealed his fate sooner, possibly, than enemy gunfire or bullets.

Jim's enterprise was concealed behind a quiet, unobtrusive manner. He was a steady young man, opposed to alcohol and tobacco but possessing an easy sense of humour that won him to his colleagues. At school he kept very much in the background, a rather over-protected child preferring to remain unnoticed. While at March he fell in love with Edna Belson of Peterborough and they became a close couple. Happily Edna was accepted and well-liked by Walter and Alice Nightall, who could be an outspoken, even brusque lady very much in charge in her home.

Inevitably stunned by Jim's death, Alice was relieved to have Edna to lean upon and the two went together to receive the posthumous awards. Alice symbolised the grieving mother at those occasions and was pounced upon by the photographers. For some four years she longed to meet the man who had retrieved her son's body from the crater and when at last she knew his name she wrote to arrange a meeting. Eric Isaacson met her on the Palace Green at Ely where he found her already waiting on a park seat holding a piece of paper with a set of questions to put to him. She wanted to be spared no detail of the discovery and was most anxious to know if Jim was dead on being found or whether he had managed to utter last words. Eric had to describe the position of the body and all else that he saw minutely and then she walked away feeling she knew all the could be known. Eric found her charming. She was stricken with arthritis but full of gratitude for his taking the time to meet her. She later heard of his forthcoming marriage and sent him a tablecloth as a gift.

Receiving her son's George Cross at Buckingham Palace, Alice needed a helping arm to ascend the steps to the King. Taking the medal securely in her painful hands she then apologised for not being able to shake hands with him, but the King smiled, took the medal back to free and clasp her hand and an equerry helped her back down the steps. Her son had died a war hero without going to war.

It was almost as if Alice Nightall did not want Littleport to share her grief. She wanted no monument to Jim there while clinging to the belief that Soham remained the shrine to his memory. Alice died on 23rd April 1967 aged 75 and Walter on 26th April 1970 aged 84, but a subsequent honour placed on their son would surely have pleased them. Her brother Charles Barber represented them at the unveiling at March station on September 28th 1981 of two new locomotives bearing the names of James Nightall and Benjamin Gimbert. Clement Freud, the Member of Parliament for the Isle of Ely, addressed the assembly, the Bishop of Ely blessed the locomotives, a Guard of Honour was provided by the United States Air Force and hymns were led by the choir of Soham Village College. Both of those locomotives were in service later that day, the first being 47579 JAMES NIGHTALL G.C. on a parcels train. A week later the Royal Train carrying Prince Charles and Princess Diane to York and its National Railway Museum was drawn by 47577 BENJAMIN GIMBERT G.C.

After long delay in respect for the views of Alice Nightall the Littleport Parish Council in association with Network Southeast decided to honour its hero by placing a plaque on Littleport Town Hall. The Littleport Society arranged an act of remembrance at the graveside of Jim Nightall at 9.30 a.m. and the plaque was unveiled at 11 a.m. on July 22nd 1992. Present were the Chairman of Littleport Parish Council, Jane Binks, the Town Clerk, Dennis Thurling, the Reverend Terry Yaroslaw of Littleport Evangelical Church where Jim Nightall attended Sunday school, the Chairman of Littleport Society, Granville Goodson, and the Public Affairs Manager for the West Anglia and Great Northern Division of British Rail's Network Southeast, Michael Lamport, who was to illustrate the structure of those bombs that disrupted Soham on June 2nd 1944.

The bereaved Alice Nightall outside her home at 15, The Hythe, Littleport 1944.

Alice Nightall, with Edna Belson, contemplates her son's George Cross outside Buckingham Palace, 10th October 1944. (Ron Barber Collection)

Charles Barber unveils the James Nightall locomotive at March Station 28th September 1981.

The new Soham. *(Author's photograph)*

The Wedding Day of Frank and May in Wisbech, 29th May 1920.
(Florence Young Collection)

FRANK CHARLES COPELAND BRIDGES (1896 — 1944)

He was born in Gayton, King's Lynn, on 25th November 1896 to Alice Louisa Bridges, later Copeland, whose other children were Truman and Florence Victoria Copeland. Her husband Frank Rightcraft Copeland was a journeyman painter and the couple lived at 9, Agenoria Street, a pleasant area near the park and St. Augustine's Church, Wisbech. After leaving school and taking what work he could Frank Bridges, at the outbreak of the first world war joined the Cambridgeshire Regiment, rose to the rank of sergeant and was wounded in action three times. Those wounds thwarted his post-war ambition to join the Metropolitan Police, for which he was otherwise eminently suitable in mind and body, being six-feet, four inches tall with a heightened sense of responsibility.

Frank joined the railways and became a porter at Wisbech. He married May Eliza Salmon of March, then living in Wisbech, on 29th May 1920 at St. Peter's Church, Wisbech. May was born on 8th January 1898 and her father, Henry Salmon was a railway guard living in a fine property at Nene Parade, March, commensurate with his responsibilities then. March gained these huge marshalling yards, which during the last war became the largest in Europe, over Wisbech because the influential landowners there, the Peckover family, were Quakers and would not release the land where it would entail working on Sundays.

Frank and May Bridges had three sons. George was born in 1922, served as a machine gunner in the Fifth Bucks and East Kent Regiment during the second world war, but was killed in action in Sicily on August 9th 1943. From its temporary grave his body was moved to Catania and there each Christmas a wreath is placed, through the British Legion, on behalf of his close friend Eric Isaacson. Dennis, the second son, worked for the railways before doing his national service as a Bevin Boy in the coal mines, after which he remained a miner, working underground for forty-four years. Gordon, the third son, remained in Soham, working for the gas company.

Frank went to sea only to get to France during his war service.

Truman was the seafarer, making it his career, but somehow the tag 'Sailor' attached itself to Frank. A warm, friendly, easy going man, Frank was greatly liked. He was an ace darts player, fond of a drink with his pals. He was appointed signalman at Snailwell Junction before moving to Soham in 1939, succeeding Walter Ayres who had retired. Frank and his family lived in Brook Street, Soham.

Just as there had been tragedy in the Gimbert family just prior to the Soham incident, so it occured in the Bridges family with the death of George on foreign soil, a fondly remembered personality. Frank died of his terrible injuries in White Lodge Hospital, Newmarket, a few hours after the explosion. His wife later married again. Largely through the persistence of Eric Isaacson a new sheltered housing development off Sand Street, Soham, was named Frank Bridges Close long after the tragedy, but he was to receive no other recognition for his part in the vital action of that night apart from being included on the commemorative plaques in Soham church and Soham Village College.

(Author's photograph)

Frank Bridges in holiday mood in the 1930s.
(Gordon Bridges' Collection)

George Bridges in KD tropical uniform.
(Eric Isaacson Collection)

Herbert Clarke in his eighties. *(Arthur Clarke Collection)*

HERBERT GEORGE CLARKE (1885 — 1976)

He was born on 24th April 1885 in Elmswell, Suffolk to Sophia Clarke, who as Sophia Gurling was to have four more children including William who died in India in 1907 and Arthur who was killed in the war in 1916, the other two being daughters. Herbert was fostered by an aunt in Elmswell, Suffolk, and his first choice of work after leaving school there was the railways.

He became a horse-boy at Ipswich station and progressed gradually to signalman. He took over the signalman's job at Thorpe le Soken near Clacton in Essex, from where he chose his bride, Alice McCullouch, who was born in 1884 in Huntingdon of Scottish descent and was then in service in Thorpe le Soken. The couple had three sons. Edward was born in 1910 and Arthur in 1920 but when it looked probable that the couple were to have no more children they adopted William, who was born in 1917.

Herbert was appointed signalman at Ipswich before advancing to become a Goods Guard, which job he held until the incident at Soham. While this inflicted no severe flesh wounds on him he was sadly reduced by the resultant shock. After returning from Ely Hospital he was propped up in bed for six months and never fully recovered his health. He returned to work to perform light duties at Ipswich station and retired a few months early in 1949 aged 64.

After losing Alice in 1956 aged 72 Herbert moved in with Edward at Severn Road, Ipswich, until he was offered a council house where he settled into a long retirement. He died there at 2, Willowcroft Road on 6th January 1976 in his 91st year and is buried in new Cemetery.

'My father,' said Arthur his son, who had pleaded in vain for some recognition for him after his part in the Soham incident, 'could talk about almost anything.' Indeed, Herbert maintained a healthy curiosity about many aspects of life to the end. For his reticence at work, however, he was known as 'Quiet Herbert.' He was no man to complain about his lot and was popular with his colleagues and loved by his sons. Herbert worked hard for his family and made full use of an allotment garden to feed them.

Of his family, Arthur followed his father into working for the railways and became a clerk at the goods yard at Ipswich. He then spent the war years in the Royal Air Force, becoming a rear gunner in Halifax bombers on night raids, leaving the Americans to raid by day. Afterwards he returned to his railway job for a while, then took a job with ICI. William became a shop steward and Edward had done war service with the Devonshire Light Infantry.

Herbert Clarke attended the unveiling of the plaque transferred from the station hut to Soham Village College on June 2nd 1966 and Arthur represented his late father at the ceremony of unveiling the locomotives at March station on September 28th 1981.

Herbert Clarke and Ben Gimbert survey the tablet in Soham Village College on 2nd June 1966. *(Arthur Clarke Collection)*

OTHERS INVOLVED:

CYRIL KING (1910 — 1981)

He was born on 18th March 1910 at Longstanton near Cambridge to Gertrude and Arthur King, a railwayman who became Railways Controller at Cambridge. The couple also had a daughter. Cyril's grandfather was also a railwayman based in Haverhill, Suffolk. Cyril was a bright scholar who won a scholarship to attend the Perse School in Cambridge, but he clung to the family fixation for railways and was happy to pursue his future there.

He married Edith Snutch of King's Cross, London, on 12th August 1939 and within the month he was given the post of signalman at Barway Junction. Edith described her husband as 'railway mad.' The couple moved to 14, Mereside, Soham from where Cyril cycled to work daily or nightly. From Barway he moved to replace Frank Bridges at Soham, using that makeshift signalling system at first, and from there he moved to Ely North Junction where he stayed until his retirement, still cycling to work from Soham. The Kings moved from Mereside to the former public house, 'The Jolly Farmers' at The Cotes and then to 9, King's Parade, Soham. Ill health forced Cyril to retire a few months early in 1974. He died on March 17th 1981, the day before his 71st birthday.

Cyril's first concern after the explosion was for the safety of his wife living so near to it, but Edith soon got the message through via Percy Leonard on his cycle, a railwayman attached to Soham station a long time, that she was safe and well. Indeed she was busy helping others worse off, using an oil stove to make tea with Ben Bradley, living opposite, supplying the milk from his own cows. Meanwhile Cyril was receiving the spent Herbert Clarke after his ordeal, helping him up the steps of his box and making him tea. He described the tea as the worst he had ever made! At the instigation of Claude Hitch, another railwayman, an ambulance arrived in case Herbert needed hospital attention. After the two ambulancemen decided this was unnecessary Cyril and Claude, who had arrived with them, persuaded them otherwise and Herbert was taken away. As it happened, Cyril should not have been on duty that night. His fellow signalman, Fred Titchmarsh, was booked for the night shift but he wanted to spend an evening with his bride to be and Cyril relented.

The Kings were not on the telephone while living at Mereside but Edith's sister in London sometimes telephoned Ben Bradley for news of them. Getting through on the day after the explosion she was told the signalman had been killed and hung up assuming it was Cyril. Seeking confirmation she was then told the truth.

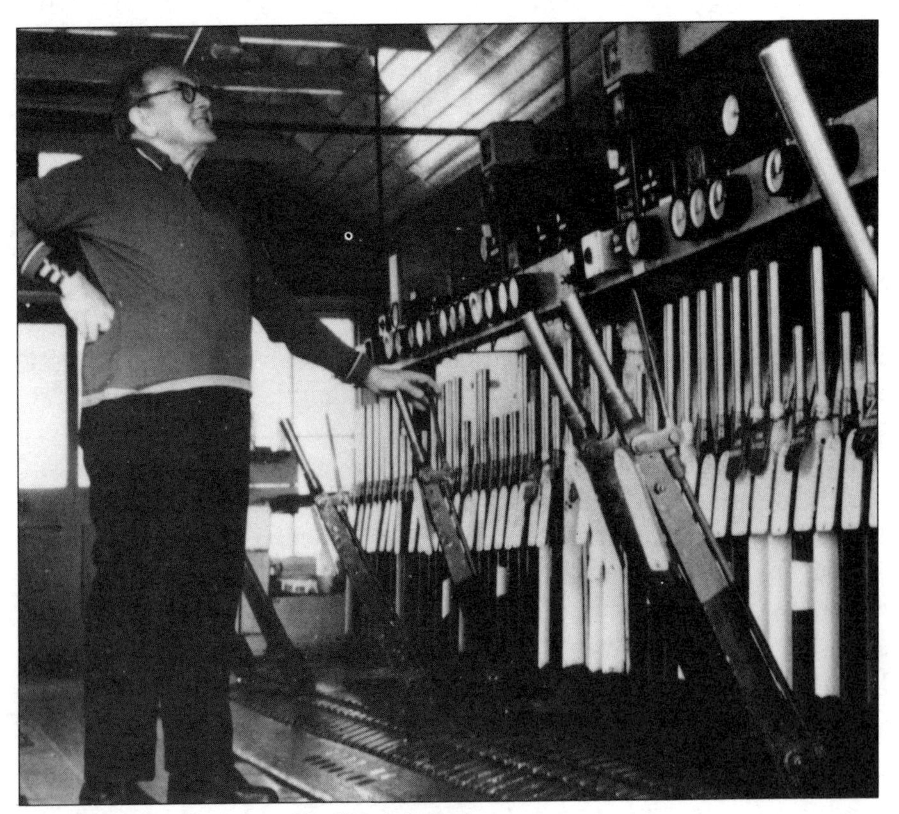

Cyril King in the box at Ely North Junction.
(Edith King Collection)

HARRY OLIVER (1896 — 1974)

While Soham rocked and splintered on the night of the blast the stationmaster's house in which Harry Oliver and his family slept came down about them. One moment he was asleep, oblivious of the drama outside, the next pinned and helpless in the dark, wondering which world he was in. They pulled Harry free just in time, for moments after he left the ruin the rest folded in. While he soon recovered in Newmarket Hospital the trauma stayed with him a long time. He resumed his role of stationmaster — without a station — at Soham and retired from there in 1961.

Harry Oliver was born in Hilgay, Norfolk, the son of a Norfolk police constable. He went to Snettisham Grammar School and served in the first world war, after which he joined the railways. He was given his first post as stationmaster at Bolingbroke in Lincolnshire and he moved to Soham as stationmaster in 1941, where he was greatly liked. After his retirement he and his wife Winifred moved to North Wootton near King's Lynn where she outlived him. Their daughter, Pat Seal, who worked at Soham station, lives in Gorleston, Norfolk, but their son Dick died a few years ago.

After wandering away to find shelter and comfort after her husband had been taken to hospital Winifred Oliver hardly had time to gather her thoughts before she had to face the fact that, due to the urgent need to restore the lines through Soham, all her furnishings that might have salvaged had been bulldozed into the crater with the rubble and she had to face the prospect of a new start with unfamiliar objects around her. Pat Oliver had been taken in by the Kings.

Winifred and Harry Oliver in Soham in 1948.
(Pat Seal Collection)

WILLIAM REED, the man who found Ben Gimbert after the explosion, was born in Soham and lived in Fountain Lane. When he retired as a Ganger he had worked for the railways for 42 years. During the second world war he was also a sergeant then sergeant-major in the Soham Home Guard, but he was not in that role when he turned out to join the chaos at the station that night. Bill Reed died aged 73. His son Dick saw active service in the navy during the second world war and is a devoted member of the British Legion.

WILLIAM FULLER, the Sub-Ganger, or Platelayer, living in the shattered Mount Pleasant cottage, who also went to hospital that night, was a Fordham man. Although big and strong Will had to attend hospital for a long time as a result of the injury he received. His daughter Connie, who with her mother survived the night relatively unscathed, married Jack Graham who became landlord of 'The Angel' in Station Road, Soham.

Soham Home Guard sitting in front of the bandstand (now demolished) in the Recreation Ground. In the front row sitting on chairs, fourth from right, is Sergeant William Reed. *(Cambridgeshire Collection)*

ERIC ISAACSON and his brother Ken succeeded into their father's butcher's trade in the shop on the corner of Bushel Lane, Hall Street, Soham. Ken has described his life as a butcher vividly in a manuscript preserved at the Cambridge Library. Eric, who on that night of fear spent tense minutes wondering if he too was about to be blown up by the locomotive's boiler or by more bombs on the detached train, became an influential figure in Soham, an MC for many a public occasion and a compere for local and neighbouring shows. In 1953 he produced 'Showtime' with a troupe of performers including 'The Toppers,' a female dancing chorus wearing what might have been the first miniskirts. The planned one-night performance in the Central Hall (formerly cinema) extended to five nights and the show went round neighbouring communities for weeks. This, of course, for Coronation year, but Eric brought the same group together for a revival of 'Showtime' in the Jubilee year of 1977 when the dancers appeared to have retained all their glamour.

Retired from his trade, Eric Isaacson today is a District Councillor. He fought hard for a long time to achieve recognition for Frank Bridges, but the powers that be would not accept the significance of his part in the incident of June 2nd 1944, claiming also that it was too long after the event to reassess his part in it. At long last, however, his name has been perpetuated by FRANK BRIDGES CLOSE in Sand Street, Soham.

(left to right), Colonel Jack Ennion, Eric Isaacson and Albert Lawrence, Head of Soham Village College, have just arrived back by rail from March station after the unveiling of the Gimbert and Nightall locomotives on 28th September 1981. The restored signal box no longer remains. *(Eric Isaacson Collection)*

The Soham bomb displayed in Littleport on 22nd July 1992.
(John W. Byrne)

To commemorate the fiftieth anniversary of the Soham explosion some pupils of Soham Village College produced this village sign incorporating the locomotive against a background of flames. It is sited in Fordham Road. (Author's photograph)

THE AUTHOR

Anthony Day is a professional landscape painter who also writes. He studied art at the Cambridge School of Art from 1948 to 1952 and at Reading University from 1954 to 1955, thereafter specialising in painting the fen country and its towns, selling his work through dealers in London and East Anglia and mixed exhibitions such as the Royal Academy and the Royal Society of British Artists.

For fourteen years he was art critic to the *'Cambridge Evening News'* but he is now principally interested in writing about country matters and local history. Recent articles by him have been published in *'The Countryman'* and *'Cambridgeshire Life.'* He has assembled a huge archive of photographs of his native village of Wicken which he has used in books, exhibitions and slide-shows and took part in the important *'Fen Archive'* exhibition at the Cambridge Darkroom gallery in 1986, the catalogue of which is now a collectors' item.